Love's Arrow

John Frederick Herring Snr. (1795-1865) *Barney, Leave the Girls Alone*

Grange BOOKS

Mary F. Raphael (fl.1889-1915) *Britomart and Amoret*

Love's Arrow

Compiled By Anna Nicholas

Hermann Koch (1856-1894) *Teatime Romance*

A selection of poems and quotations

The Publishers would like to acknowledge the following
for permission to reproduce copyright material:
Page 14, The Macmillan Company for 'When You Are
Old and Grey' by W.B. Yeats, from The Collected Poems
of W.B. Yeats; Page 29, The Macmillan Company for
'She Wore a New
'Terracotta' Dress' by Thomas Hardy; Page 30, Roger
Mc Gough and Jonathan Cape Ltd for 'My Cat and I' by
Roger McGough.

The Publishers have made every effort to trace coyright
holders of material reproduced within this compilation.
If, however, they have inadvertanly made any error
they would be grateful for notification.

Many thanks to Paperchase, London for kindly allowing
us to use their papers.

Pictures courtesy of The Bridgeman Art Library.   The
Three Ages of Man by Titian; collection of the Duke of
Sutherland, on loan to the Gallery of Scotland.

Pictures courtesy of The Bridgeman Art Library

Published in 1995 by
Grange Books
An imprint of Grange Books PLC
The Grange, Grange Yard
London SE1 3AG

Copyright © 1994 Regency House Publishing Limited

ISBN 1 85627 631 7

Auguste Rodin (1840-1917) *The Kiss*

Walter Crane (1845-1915) *La Belle Dame Sans Merci*

O, Love, love, love!

Love is like a dizziness;

It winna let a poor body

Gang about his biziness!

James Hogg 1770-1835

Theodor Kleehaus (b.1854) *The Proposal*

Love
and a
cough
cannot
be hid.

Latin proverb

Eugene de Blaas (b.1843) *The Fisherman's Wooing*

St Catherine, St Catherine,
O lend me thine aid,
And grant that I never
may die an old maid.
A husband, St Catherine,
A **good** one, St Catherine;
But arn-a-one better than
Narn-a-one, St Catherine.

Sweet St Catherine,
A husband, St Catherine,
Handsome, St Catherine,
Rich, St Catherine.

Anon

Marcus Stone (1840-1921) *Il y en toujours un autre*.

*L*ove does not consist of gazing at each other but in looking outward together in the same direction.

A. de Saint-Exupery

William Hatherell (19th century) *Tess of the D'Urbevilles: The Elopement*

William Mulready (1786-1863) *First Love*

'Tis easy enough to be twenty-one:

'Tis easy enough to marry;

But when you try both games at once

'Tis a bloody big load to carry.

Anon

Cesare-Auguste Detti (1847-1914) *The Courtship*

11

She walks in beauty, like the night
Of cloudless climes and starry skies;
And all that's best of dark and bright
Meet in her aspect and her eyes.

From: *She Walks in Beauty*. Lord Byron 1788-1824

William Dyce (1806-1864) *Francesca da Rimini*

12

Titian (c.1485-1576) *The Three Ages of Man* (detail)

Love seeketh not itself to please,

Nor for itself hath any care,

But for another gives its ease,

And builds a Heaven in Hell's despair.

William Blake 1757-1827

13

When you are old and grey and full of sleep,

And nodding by the fire, take down this book,

And slowly read, and dream of the soft look

Your eyes had once, and of their shadows deep;

How many loved your moments of glad grace,

And loved your beauty with love false or true,

But one man loved the pilgrim soul in you,

And loved the sorrows of your changing face;

And bending down beside the glowing bars,

Murmur, a little sadly, how Love fled

And paced upon the mountains overhead

And hid his face amid a crown of stars.

W.B. Yeats 1865-1939

14

Francis Danby (1793-1861) *Disappointed Love*

The night has a thousand eyes,
  And the day but one;
Yet the light of the bright world dies
  With the dying sun.

The mind has a thousand eyes,
  And the heart but one;
Yet the light of a whole life dies
  When love is done.

Francis William Bourdillon 1852-1921

15

*Heaven has
no rage like love
to hatred turned,
Nor hell a fury
like a woman
scorned.*

William Congreve 1670-1729

16

Arturo Ricci (b.1854) *The Quarrel*

John Seymour Lucus (1849-1923) *The Flirtation*

Although I conquer all the earth,
Yet for me there is only one city.
In that city there is for me only one house;
And in that house, one room only;
And in that room, a bed.
And one woman sleeps there,
The shining joy and jewel of all my kingdom.

Ancient Indian

17

How do I love thee? Let me count the ways.

I love thee to the depth and breadth and height

My soul can reach, when feeling out of sight

For the ends of Being and ideal Grace.

I love thee to the level of every day's

Most quiet need, by sun and candlelight.

I love thee freely, as men strive for Right;

I love thee purely, as they turn from Praise.

I love thee with the passion put to use

In my old griefs, and with my childhood's faith.

I love thee with a love I seemed to lose

With my lost saints, – I love thee with the breath,

Smiles, tears, of all my life! – and, if God choose,

I shall but love thee better after death.

Elizabeth Barrett Browning 1806-1861

Love is a springtime
plant that perfumes
everything with its hope,
even the ruins to which
it clings.

Gustave Flaubert 1821-1880

Giovanni-Battista Tiepolo (1696-1770) *Rinaldo and Armida*

Love comes in at the window
and goes out through the door.

Camden 1614

Eugene de Blaas (b.1843) *On the Balcony*

20

William Henry Fisk (1827-1884) *The Secret*

Shall I compare thee to a summer's day?

Thou art more lovely and more temperate:

Rough winds do shake the darling buds of May,

And summer's lease hath all too short a date:

Sometime too hot the eye of heaven shines,

And often is his gold complexion dimmed;

And every fair from fair sometime declines,

By chance, or nature's changing course untrimmed;

But thy eternal summer shall not fade,

Nor lose possession of that fair thou owest,

Nor shall death brag thou wanderest in his shade,

When in eternal lines to time thou growest;

So long as men can breathe, or eyes can see,

So long lives this, and this gives life to thee.

William Shakespeare 1564-1616

Drink to me only with thine eyes,
  And I will pledge with mine;
Or leave a kiss but in the cup
  And I'll not look for wine.
The thirst that from the soul doth rise
  Doth ask a drink divine;
But I might of Jove's nectar sup,
  I would not change for thine.

I sent thee late a rosy wreath,
  Not so much honouring thee
As giving it a hope that there
  It would not withered be;
But thou thereon didst only breathe,
  And sent'st it back to me;
Since when it grows, and smells, I swear,
  Not of itself but thee!

Ben Jonson 1572-1637

Alfred W. Elmore (1815-1881) *A Greek Ode*

22

Haynes King (1831-1904) *Jealousy and Flirtation*

All is fair in love and war.

Proverb 17th C

23

Remember me when I am gone away,
  Gone far away into the silent land;
    When you can no more hold me by the hand,
Nor I half turn to go, yet turning stay.
Remember me when no more day by day
  You tell me of our future that you planned:
    Only remember me; you understand
It will be late to counsel then or pray.

Yet if you should forget me for a while
  And afterwards remember, do not grieve:
    For if the darkness and corruption leave
    A vestige of the thoughts that once I had,
Better by far you should forget and smile
  Than that you should remember and be sad.

Christina Rossetti 1830-1894

H. Zatzka (b.1859) *The Rose Bower*

24

Angelica Kauffman (1741-1807) *Abelard Soliciting the Hand of Helouise*

Absence sharpens love,
presence strengthens it.

Fuller, 1732

25

She stood in her scarlet gown,
If any one touched her
The gown rustled.
Eia.
She stood, her face like a rose,
Shining she stood
And her mouth was a flower.
Eia.
She stood by the branch of a tree,
And writ her love on a leaf.

From: *Carmina Burana* 12th C.

François Boucher (1703-1770) *Landscape with Figures Gathering Cherries*

William Holman Hunt (1827-1910) *The Awakening Conscience*

I wish I could remember that first day,
First hour, first moment of your meeting me,
If bright or dim the season, it might be
Summer or Winter for aught I can say;
So unrecorded did it slip away,
So blind was I to see and to foresee,
So dull to mark the budding of my tree
That would not blossom yet for many a May.
If only I could recollect it, such
A day of days! I let it come and go
As traceless as the thaw of bygone snow;
It seemed to mean so little, meant so much;
If only now I could recall that touch,
First touch of hand in hand — Did one but know!

Christina Rossetti 1830-1894

In the Spring a young man's fancy lightly turns to thoughts of love.

Alfred, Lord Tennyson 1809-1892

Theodore Blake Wirgman (1848-1925) *Gather Ye Rosebuds While Ye May*

She wore a new 'terra-cotta' dress,
And she stayed, because of the pelting storm,
Within the hansom's dry recess,
Though the horse had stopped; yea motionless
  We sat on, snug and warm.

Then the downpour ceased, to my sharp sad pain
And the glass that had screened our forms before
Flew up, and out she sprang to her door:
I should have kissed her if the rain
  Had lasted a minute more.

Thomas Hardy 1840-1928

Maurice Chabas (1862-1947) *Sunday*

29

Girls are simply the prettiest things
My cat and I believe
And we're always saddened
When it's time for them to leave

We watch them titivating
(that often takes a while)
And though they keep us waiting
My cat & I just smile

We like to see them to the door
Say how sad it couldn't last
Then my cat and I go back inside
And talk about the past.

Roger McGough

Povl Steffensen (1866-1923) *By the Sea*

She dwelt among the untrodden ways

   Beside the springs of Dove,

A maid whom there were none to praise

   And very few to love:

A violet by a mossy stone

   Half hidden from the eye!

– Fair as a star, when only one

   Is shining in the sky.

She lived unknown, and few could know

   When Lucy ceased to be;

But she is in her grave, and, oh,

   The difference to me!

William Wordsworth 1770-1850

31

What men call gallantry,

and gods adultery,

Is much more common

where the climate's sultry.

Lord Byron 1788-1824

Walter Richard Sickert (1860-1942) *The Lovers*

Pal Szintei Merse (1845-1920) *The Lovers*

If thou remember'st not the slightest folly
That ever love did make thee run into,
Thou hast not loved.

From: *As You Like It*. William Shakespeare 1564-1616

33

Jenny kiss'd me when we met,

Jumping from the chair she sat in;

Time, you thief, who love to get

Sweets into your list, put that in!

Say I'm weary, say I'm sad,

Say that health and wealth have missed me,

Say I'm growing old, but add,

Jenny kiss'd me.

Leigh Hunt 1784-1859

Frederick Morgan (1856-1927) *The Rivals*

René Bull (d.1942) *Ruba'iyat of Omar Khayyam: A Love*

You rising moon that looks for us again –
How oft hereafter will she wax and wane;
    How oft hereafter rising look for us
Through this same Garden – and for <u>one</u> in vain!

From: *Omar Khayyam*. Edward Fitzgerald 1809-1883

35

John J. Lee (fl. 1850-1860) *Sweethearts and Wives*

Do you think your mother
and I should have liv'd
comfortably so long
together, if ever we had
been married?

From: *The Beggar's Opera*. John Gay 1685-1732

Stay, O Sweet, and do not rise,
   The light that shines comes from thine eyes;
   The day breaks not, it is my heart,
Because that you and I must part.
   Stay, or else my joys will die,
   And perish in their infancy.

Anon. 16th C.

John Ballantyne (1815-1897) *The Artist and His Model*

Roses are red, my love
Violets are blue
Sugar is sweet, my love
But not so sweet as you.

Isaac Snowman (fl. 1900-1920) *A Letter of Love*

James Archer (1824-1904) *Robert Burns and Highland Mary*

O my Luve's like a red, red rose,
　　That's newly sprung in June;
O my Luve's like the melodie
　　That's sweetly play'd in tune. —

As fair thou art, my bonie lass,
　　So deep in luve am I;
And I will love thee still, my Dear,
　　Till a' the seas gang dry. —

Till a' the seas gang dry, my Dear,
　　And the rocks melt wi' the sun:
I will love thee still, my Dear,
　　While the sands o' life shall run. —

And fare thee weel, my only Luve!
　　And fare thee weel, a while!
And I will come again, my Luve,
　　Tho' it were ten thousand mile!

Robert Burns 1759–1796

A flower was offered to me,

Such a flower as May never bore;

But I said 'I've a Pretty Rose-tree,'

And passed the sweet flower o'er.

Then I went to my Pretty Rose-tree,

To tend her day and by night;

But my Rose turned away with jealousy,

And her thorns were my only delight.

William Blake 1757-1827

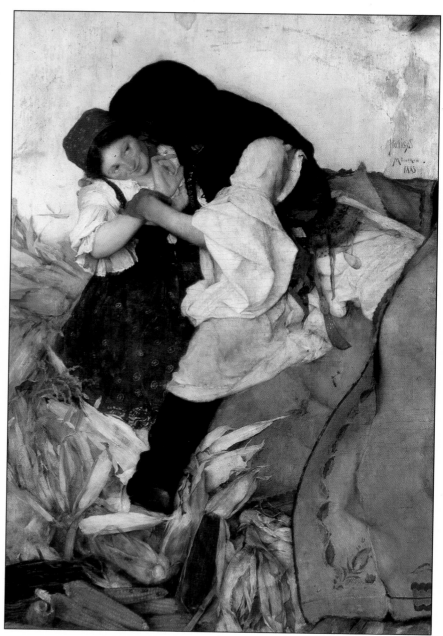

Simon Hollosy (1857-1918) *Husking Corn*

40

Love
makes
the
world
go
round.

Proverb 17th C

Joseph Frederick Soulacroix (1825-1897) *The Embrace*

It is the evening hour,
  How silent all doth lie,
The horned moon he shows his face
  In the river with the sky.
Just by the path on which we pass,
  The flaggy lake lies still as glass.

Spirit of her I love,
  Whispering to me,
Stories of sweet visions, as I rove,
  Here stop, and crop with me
Sweet flowers that in the still hour grew,
We'll take them home, nor shake off the bright dew.

Mary, or sweet spirit of thee,
  As the bright sun shines tomorrow.
Thy dark eyes these flowers shall see,
  Gathered by me in sorrow.
In the still hour when my mind was free
To walk alone – yet wish I walked with thee.

John Clare 1793-1864

Jean-Baptiste Joseph Pater (1695-1736) *The Swing*

42

François Boucher (1703-1770) *Man.Offering Grapes to a Girl*

L et us use it while we may.
Snatch those joys that haste away!
Earth her winter coat may cast,
And renew her beauty past:
But, our winter come, in vain
We solicit spring again;
And when our furrows snow shall cover,
Love may return but never lover.

Of Beauty. Sir Richard Fanshawe 1608-1666

Love is blind.

Proverb 14th C

Sir Frank Dicksee (1853-1928) *The Confession*

44

Johann Kurtwell (mid-19th century) *Lovers in the Kitchen*

I will make my kitchen, and you shall keep your room,

Where white flows the river and bright blows the broom,

And you shall wash your linen and keep your body white

In rainfall at morning and dewfall at night.

And this shall be for music when no one else is near,

The fine song for singing, the rare song to hear!

That only I remember, that only you admire,

Of the broad road that stretches and the roadside fire.

Robert Louis Stevenson 1850-1894

45

My heart still hovering round about you,

I thought I could not live without you;

Now we have lived three months asunder

How I lived with you is the wonder.

Robert, Earl Nugent

William Hogarth (1697-1764) *Marriage à la Mode – Shortly After the Marriage*

I remember the way we parted,
  The day and the way we met;
You hoped we were both broken-hearted,
  And knew we should both forget.

And the best and the worst of this is
  That neither is most to blame,
If you have forgotten my kisses,
  And I have forgotten your name.

Algernon Swinburne 1837-1909

Robert Collinson (fl. 1854-1890) *Farewell to the Light Brigade*

47

Love is a circle that doth restless move
In the same sweet eternity of love.

Robert Herrick 1591-1674

Henri de Toulouse-Lautrec (1864-1901) *In Bed*